MASSACHUSETTS

Past and Present

Jeri Freedman

rosen publishing's
rosen
central®

New York

Published in 2010 by The Rosen Publishing Group, Inc.
29 East 21st Street, New York, NY 10010

Library of Congress Cataloging-in-Publication Data

Freedman, Jeri.
Massachusetts: past and present / Jeri Freedman.—1st ed.
    p. cm.—(The United States: past and present)
Includes bibliographical references and index.
ISBN-13: 978-1-4358-5294-5 (library binding)
ISBN-13: 978-1-4358-5586-1 (pbk)
ISBN-13: 978-1-4358-5587-8 (6 pack)
1. Massachusetts—Juvenile literature. I. Title.
F64.3.F74 2010
974.4—dc22

2008054229

Manufactured in the United States of America

On the cover: Top left: A nineteenth-century engraving of British troops evacuating Boston in 1776. Top right: The Boston skyline. Bottom: The town of Provincetown, located on Cape Cod.

Contents

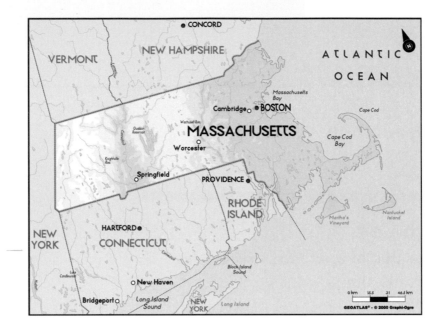

Massachusetts is in New England, north of Connecticut and south of New Hampshire and Vermont. Nantucket and Martha's Vineyard islands are off Cape Cod in the Atlantic.

Introduction

Massachusetts is located in the northeast corner of the United States. It is one of six states that make up New England, an area so named because immigrants from England settled there originally.

Massachusetts is bordered on the east by the Atlantic Ocean, on the north by New Hampshire and Vermont, on the south by Connecticut and Rhode Island, and on the west by New York. The state of Massachusetts covers approximately 7,840 square miles (20,306 square kilometers) of land and another 2,715 square miles (7,032 sq km) of water.

One of the original thirteen colonies, Massachusetts played a key role in the American Revolution. Today, it is a center for a number of major industries, including health care, education, and technology. A number of "firsts" have taken place in Massachusetts, starting with the first Thanksgiving in 1621. In 1634, the Boston Common became the first public park in America. In 1636, the first college in America, Harvard, was founded in what is now Cambridge. In 1638, the first American printing press was set up in Cambridge, and in 1653, the first public library in America opened in Boston. In 1780, Massachusetts became the first state to draft a written constitution. In 1831, William Lloyd Garrison began publishing the first abolitionist (antislavery) newspaper, *The Liberator*. In 1898, the first subway in the United States opened in Boston.

Chapter 1

The Geography of Massachusetts

Massachusetts has many different types of terrain, from the coastline on its eastern edge to the Berkshire Mountains in the western part of the state. The coast is made up of a series of bays, with terrain consisting of rocky shoreline, marshes, and rolling hills. At the southeastern tip of Massachusetts is the resort area of Cape Cod. South of Cape Cod are the islands of Nantucket and Martha's Vineyard and a number of smaller barrier islands. The bays of Massachusetts contain the state's major ports, including Gloucester, Salem, and New Bedford. In earlier times, merchant ships, fishing boats, and whalers sailed from these ports. They are still home to fishing fleets, as well as centers of shipping commerce, in the state.

The central and western parts of Massachusetts are mostly rural areas. Mountains cover the western part of the state. Along the Massachusetts–New York border lie the Taconic Mountains. These contain Mt. Greylock, the highest mountain in Massachusetts, at 3,491 feet (1,064 meters) above sea level. Another well-known mountain is Mt. Wachusett, in central Massachusetts, with an elevation of 2,000 feet (611 m). The Berkshire Mountains extend down from the Green Mountains in Vermont through northwestern Massachusetts. The Berkshires are separated from the Taconic Mountains by the Housatonic-Hoosic Valley, through which the

The foliage in the Berkshire Mountains is spectacular when the trees change color in the fall. Viewing foliage is a major draw for tourists in the autumn.

The Back Bay

The city of Boston looks a lot different today than when it was first settled. One major change involved the creation of the Back Bay neighborhood. Today, the Back Bay covers land bordered by the Charles River, Boylston Street, Dartmouth Street, and Arlington Street. Prior to 1857, however, this area was underwater. The Charles River ran into a large bay that separated Boston from Cambridge. In 1814, the Boston and Roxbury Mill Corporation built a dam in the bay and constructed a toll road linking Boston to Watertown, to the west. The dam turned the Back Bay into a series of tidal flats, which smelled unpleasant in the summer heat. The state of Massachusetts, which owned the land under the bay, felt it could develop the area to raise money and make it more attractive. In 1857, construction began, with the Charles River Railroad Company filling in the area with gravel quarried in the town of Needham, 9 miles (14 km) away. After laying out the streets, the state sold lots, raising $4 million—a large sum at the time.

Today, the Back Bay includes an area of elegant nineteenth-century townhouses on Beacon Street, Marlborough Street, and Commonwealth Avenue, as well as the upscale shopping district on Newbury and Boylston Streets. In the center of the Back Bay is Commonwealth Avenue. A tree-lined mall runs down the length of the avenue, ending at the Boston Public Garden, a formal city park.

Victorian brownstones line the streets of the Back Bay Street.

Hoosic River runs. The Connecticut River runs through the part of the Connecticut River Valley that extends into western Massachusetts. The largest body of water in Massachusetts, the man-made Quabbin Reservoir, is located in west-central Massachusetts. It provides Boston and many other municipalities with drinking water.

The east coast of Massachusetts is heavily populated with cities and towns. The largest is the state capital, Boston. The southern side of Boston is surrounded by the Great Blue Hills. The tallest point, Great Blue Hill, is 635 feet (194 m) high.

Climate

The state has a temperate climate. Because of its proximity to the sea, eastern Massachusetts is humid. Winters are cold, with January being the coldest month. Temperatures in January average 22 degrees Fahrenheit (−6 degrees Celsius) but can drop below 0°F (-18°C). Summers are hot, with temperatures averaging 82°F (28°C) in July but sometimes reaching 100°F (38°C) or higher. Precipitation (rain and snow) levels are stable across the state and the seasons, ranging from 3 to 4 inches (7.5 to 10 centimeters) per month.

Plant and Animal Life of Massachusetts

Massachusetts has two major types of wildlife habitat: forest and coastal. At one time, practically the whole state was covered by forest. Over time, however, much of this woodland was cut down for farmland and cities. Nevertheless, there is still a large amount of forest in Massachusetts. This provides a home to many animals, including white-tailed deer, raccoons, squirrels, mice, skunks, beavers, ducks, geese, wild turkeys, and hawks. In the less populous areas of central and western Massachusetts, black bears are found as well.

The marshes and shore provide a habitat for sea birds like seagulls and terns. The Cape Cod area is home to dolphins and several varieties of whales. (Whale-watching boat trips are popular in the summer.)

A number of animals that used to be common in Massachusetts are now endangered species. These include the sea turtle, bald eagle, gray wolf, piping plover, curlew, puma (cougar), and whales (blue, humpback, finback, and right). The state has habitat-purchasing and conservation programs to protect habitats in which endangered animals live.

Natural Resources

Massachusetts does not have significant precious metal mining. However, it does have small deposits of copper, silver, gold, and other metals, as well as deposits of other useful materials. In central Massachusetts, there are several types of marble. Granite is produced by quarries that are primarily located in the southeastern part of the state. In addition, the state produces clay, sand, and lime, used in building and industry.

Major Cities

Massachusetts has a population of about 6.4 million people. The state is divided into fourteen counties, which are further divided into 351 cities and towns. The largest city is Boston, located on the Charles River, at the innermost point of Massachusetts Bay. Boston proper has a population of about 600,000 people. The Boston metropolitan

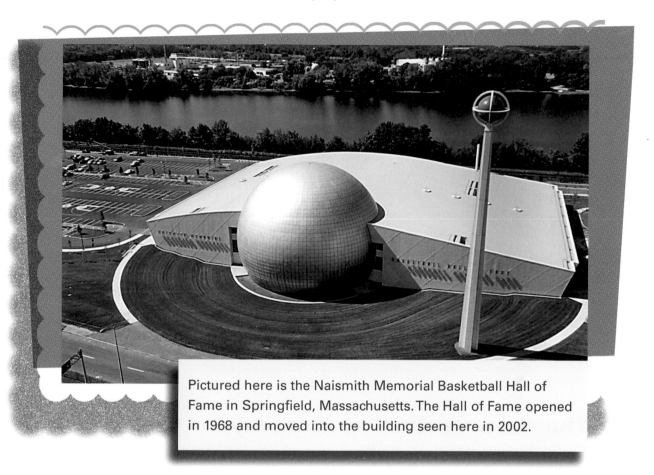

Pictured here is the Naismith Memorial Basketball Hall of Fame in Springfield, Massachusetts. The Hall of Fame opened in 1968 and moved into the building seen here in 2002.

area has a population of about 3.5 million people. The second-largest city is Worcester (pop. 172,500), in central Massachusetts. The third-largest city is Springfield (pop. 152,000), in southwestern Massachusetts.

Chapter 2

THE HISTORY OF MASSACHUSETTS

Before any Europeans came to Massachusetts, it was home to various Native American peoples. There were the Manicam in western Massachusetts, the Nauset on Cape Cod, the Nipmuc in the center of the state, the Pennacook in northeastern Massachusetts, the Pocomtuc in the northwest, and the Wampanoag in the southeast.

The Colonization of Massachusetts

The Pilgrims, from England, were the first European settlers in Massachusetts. They belonged to a religious sect that differed in its beliefs from the mainstream Church of England. Because they were persecuted in England, they sought a place where they could live according to their own religious beliefs. On September 16, 1620, the Pilgrims set out on a ship called the *Mayflower*. They intended to settle in the established English colony of Virginia. However, the weather was stormy, and the ship was blown off course. On November 19, 1620, the *Mayflower* landed on the coast of Massachusetts, near Cape Cod. There, the passengers established a small settlement. During that first winter, half the colonists died from disease, accident, or exposure, and it seemed unlikely that the colony would survive.

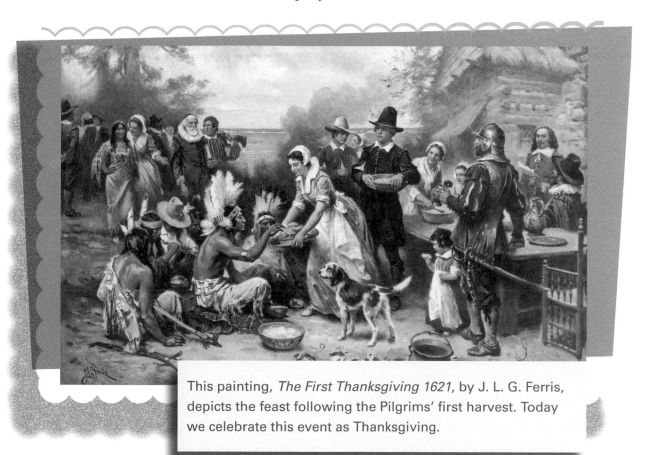

This painting, *The First Thanksgiving 1621*, by J. L. G. Ferris, depicts the feast following the Pilgrims' first harvest. Today we celebrate this event as Thanksgiving.

Massasoit, chief of the local Wampanoag Indians, thought the English colonists would be useful allies in his fight against the Narragansett Indians of present-day Rhode Island. Therefore, he helped the colonists survive. Among other things, the Wampanoag taught the Pilgrims how to grow native crops, such as corn, beans, and squash.

In 1628, a second major group of colonists arrived from England. These were the Puritans, another religious group frustrated by persecution. A group of Puritan businessmen formed the Massachusetts Bay Company. In 1629, they founded a colony in Massachusetts Bay on the Shawmut Peninsula (now Boston). There, they hoped to profit from the area's natural resources, including furs, which they traded, and wood, which they sold to shipbuilders in England.

The colonists prospered and formed new towns. By the 1690s, the Massachusetts Bay Colony claimed areas of present-day New Hampshire, Vermont, and Maine. Its population had grown to between fifty thousand and sixty thousand people.

Massachusetts in the Eighteenth Century: The Revolutionary War

In 1760, King George III came to the throne in England. He felt that the colonies were becoming too independent, and he needed money to pay off England's debts. He put a series of taxes on items that the colonists imported from England. One example was the Stamp Tax, which was applied to paper used for documents. These taxes caused a furor in the colonies. When the colonists in Boston and the surrounding cities resisted tax after tax, the English king sent soldiers to Massachusetts.

The Revolutionary War began in Massachusetts. On April 18, 1775, colonial spies observed that British soldiers were getting boats ready to leave Boston via the Charles River. Paul Revere, a silversmith and engraver, and William Dawes, a local shoemaker, took off on horses to warn the rebels who were hiding in Lexington, a town northwest of Boston. The colonial volunteer militia was known as the Minutemen because its members agreed to meet at a minute's notice. The Minutemen met the British forces at Lexington, firing the first shots of the war.

One of the most famous battles of the Revolutionary War was the Battle of Bunker Hill, which took place on the Charlestown peninsula. On June 16, 1775, the militia, led by Colonel William Prescott, went to fortify Bunker Hill. Prescott fortified nearby Breed's Hill instead, but the ensuing battle is still referred to as the Battle of Bunker Hill. More than 1,000 English soldiers and 441 colonists died in the battle.

The war spread through all thirteen colonies and continued for almost eight years. Ships built in Massachusetts formed the major part of the Continental navy, and the state supplied another 1,600 ships to be used as privateers, ships authorized by the government to attack enemy vessels.

This statue of Paul Revere is in Boston's North End, not far from the Old North Church where the arrival of the British was signaled.

On August 30, 1781, with the assistance of the French, the English colonists defeated the head of British forces in America, Lord Cornwallis, at Yorktown, Virginia. A few months later, England entered

This painting of John Hancock by George Peter Alexander Healy shows him signing the Declaration of Independence on July 4, 1776.

into peace negotiations with the colonists. John Adams of Massachusetts played a key diplomatic role in these negotiations. On November 30, 1782, the British and the English colonists signed a tentative peace treaty in Paris. It was finalized in April 1783.

In 1787, the Constitutional Convention was held in Philadelphia, Pennsylvania. John Hancock who was from Massachusetts and was president of the Continental Congress, presided over the meeting. At this meeting, the U.S. Constitution was drawn up. It contained the rules that would govern the new country. Each state had to ratify (formally accept) the constitution. So in January 1788, there was a convention in Massachusetts to consider it. The Massachusetts delegates refused to ratify the Constitution unless a series of amendments was added to protect citizens' rights. These became the Bill of Rights—the first ten amendments to the Constitution.

Massachusetts in the Nineteenth Century

Massachusetts was always a prosperous manufacturing and trading community. So it embraced the Industrial Revolution in the

Education in Colonial Times

Much of today's education is general. It focuses on developing students' ability to think and analyze, and on increasing their knowledge of the world. In addition, a great deal of what students learn is aimed at preparing them for college, where they will gain the knowledge that they need for a career.

In contrast, most education in colonial America was practical. Girls learned how to cook, make clothes, and spin wool into thread to weave cloth. Boys learned how to farm, hunt, and fish. In addition, they were often apprenticed at a young age to learn a trade, such as blacksmithing or carpentry.

Life in colonial Massachusetts revolved around religion. For example, Sunday was devoted to religious services and reading the Bible. Because it was so important to be able to read the Bible, education was important to the Puritans. Children received some basic instruction in reading at home or in small groups when they were six to eight years old. Girls were taught some reading and basic arithmetic so that they could deal with household finances, but they usually did not receive further schooling. It was assumed that they would run a household, not take up a trade or profession. Boys, on the other hand, went on to grammar schools, where they improved their skills in reading, spelling, writing, and arithmetic. Harvard College, established in 1636, provided schoolmasters for these grammar schools. Many boys left school to learn a trade. Others entered Harvard College to prepare for a career as a minister or lawyer.

nineteenth century. During this time, people began using machines to produce goods that were previously made by hand. Instead of making items at home in cottage industries, more and more workers were employed in factories. Major industries grew rapidly, including the production of iron goods, shipbuilding, paper making, publishing, and furniture making.

In 1813, a group of Boston businessmen led by Francis Cabot Lowell set up the first modern textile mill. Built in Waltham, Massachusetts, the mill used water wheels and the Charles River to power automated looms to make cloth from yarn. Other mills followed, and for decades after, Massachusetts was a center of textile manufacturing.

The Civil War

In the 1800s, Massachusetts became a center of antislavery activity. In 1832, abolitionist William Lloyd Garrison started the New England Anti-Slavery Society. Massachusetts fought on the side of the Union during the Civil War. In February 1863, President Abraham Lincoln issued a call for troops to join the Union army. In response, Governor John A. Andrew of Massachusetts ordered the organization of the first black regiment, the 54th Massachusetts Volunteer Infantry Regiment. The regiment fought in a number of campaigns over the next two years before being released from duty in 1865. A monument to the regiment can be seen today on the Boston Common.

Massachusetts in the Twentieth Century

In the early twentieth century, Massachusetts was a manufacturing center. It was also home to a prosperous fishing industry. In the late nineteenth and early twentieth centuries, immigrants from Europe had provided a steady source of cheap labor. Large groups of immigrants included the Irish, French-Canadians, Russian Jews, Italians, Scandinavians, Chinese, and Portuguese. Boston's North End became home to large numbers of Italians, while the Irish

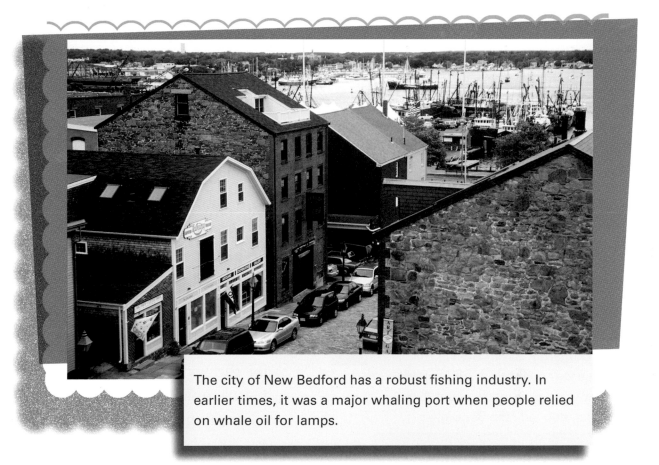

The city of New Bedford has a robust fishing industry. In earlier times, it was a major whaling port when people relied on whale oil for lamps.

settled in South Boston and the Chinese settled in Chinatown, at the edge of downtown Boston. Many of the Portuguese populated southern coastal towns like New Bedford, where they started prosperous fishing businesses.

By the middle of the 1900s, the manufacturing industry of Massachusetts began to suffer because of competition from cheaper goods from other parts of the United States, such as the South. The Great Depression, a major economic crisis caused by the collapse of the banks in 1929, finished off the textile industry in Massachusetts.

World War II and Beyond

The Leonard P. Zakim Bunker Hill Bridge was built as part of Boston's twenty-first-century transportation project, dubbed "the Big Dig,"

During World War II, a number of military air bases were built throughout Massachusetts. They were primarily used to train crews that flew fighters and bombers during the war. Shipyards in Massachusetts, such as the Fore River Shipyard in Quincy, turned out ships for the war effort as well. Massachusetts developed a booming defense industry, supplying equipment to the military during the war. Among the companies involved in the war effort was Raytheon, which played a key role in the development of radar. The deep involvement of Massachusetts in the development of new materials and technologies for the war laid the foundation for its emergence as a leader in the new field of electronics following the end of World War II.

After the war, manufacturing in Massachusetts continued to decline. However, the large number of research and educational facilities in Boston helped it make the transition to new high-technology industries.

Chapter 3

THE GOVERNMENT OF MASSACHUSETTS

Massachusetts is technically a commonwealth. There are three other commonwealths in the United States: Virginia, Pennsylvania, and Kentucky. Today, there is no difference between a commonwealth and any other type of state. However, when America was first being settled, the term indicated a colony in which the people elected their own government. In contrast, many other British colonies were governed by a royal governor appointed by the king of England.

Since 1780, the government of Massachusetts has been divided into three branches: executive, legislative, and judicial.

The Executive Branch

The executive branch consists of the governor and a number of other officials. The governor is the highest official in the state. He is assisted by a lieutenant governor, who is also an elected official, and a cabinet. The cabinet is appointed by the governor and is composed of officials called secretaries. They are responsible for overseeing specific state agencies, such as health and human services, energy, and environmental affairs. The governor also has a group of elected advisors called the Governor's Council.

The Massachusetts State House *(above)* was designed around 1795. The Latin on the state seal *(right)* says "Seal of the Republic of Massachusetts."

These other officials are part of the executive branch:

- The attorney general is responsible for seeing that crimes are prosecuted.
- The auditor makes sure that the state's money is being properly spent and accounted for.
- The treasurer and receiver general is responsible for tax collection and managing the state's finances.
- The secretary of the commonwealth oversees elections and manages the state's records divisions, such as the registry of deeds, the state bookstore, the Massachusetts Archives, and the Citizen Information Service.

Boston Politics from the Nineteenth Century Onward

Prior to 1850, Boston's leaders came primarily from powerful old families of English Protestant stock. They were referred to as the "Boston Brahmins" because they were the ruling class, like the brahmins of India.

But in the middle of the nineteenth century, one of the largest groups to immigrate to Boston was the Irish Catholics. They were fleeing the devastating potato famine in Ireland (1845–1851) and persecution by the English. They faced discrimination in Boston as well, but by the 1860s, the children of these immigrants began to challenge the old families for political power. One of the first was John F. Fitzgerald, a newspaper publisher who ran for mayor in 1905 on the Democratic ticket and won. He was succeeded in 1913 by another Irishman, James Michael Curley. Curley won by largely ignoring the powerful old families and appealing directly to the people. By the 1920s, the Irish Democrats had established a stranglehold on the political scene in Boston and paved the way for the rise of political dynasties like the Kennedys. President John F. Kennedy was a descendant of two Irish ward bosses, men who ran a particular voting district.

The Irish influence in Boston politics has continued to the present day. Among the notable Irish American politicians of recent times are Raymond Flynn, mayor of Boston from 1984 to 1993, and William Bulger, president of the Massachusetts State Senate from 1978 to 1996. Other prominent Irish American politicians from Massachusetts include senators Ted Kennedy and John Kerry.

The Legislative Branch

The legislative branch is responsible for making laws. The formal name of the Massachusetts legislature is the General Court, which it has been called since colonial times. The legislature consists of two houses: a 40-member Senate and a 160-member House of Representatives. Both senators and representatives are elected to two-year terms. The legislature contains twenty-six committees working in specific areas, such as taxes or health care. Massachusetts citizens can observe the legislature and committees at work.

The Judicial Branch

The judicial branch is the court system. It consists of three main branches: the trial court, the appeals court, and the Massachusetts Supreme Judicial Court. The trial court is responsible for judging

The Massachusetts Supreme Judicial Court and Court of Appeals are both housed in the John Adams Courthouse. The building also houses the country's oldest law library.

criminal and civil cases. Criminal cases are those that involve a crime and are prosecuted by a prosecutor from the state's attorney general's office. Civil cases are those in which one person or organization sues another. The trial court is further divided into courts that handle specific types of cases, such as the criminal court, family court (which deals with issues like custody of children), land court, juvenile court, housing court, and probate court (which deals with wills and inheritance). A person who has evidence that the judgment handed down in trial court is unfair or inappropriate can appeal the decision in the appeals court. In the appeals court, a three-judge panel reviews cases and decides whether to uphold or overturn decisions.

The Massachusetts Supreme Judicial Court was established in 1692. It enforces the Massachusetts state constitution, which was written in 1780 and is the oldest continuously used constitution in the Western Hemisphere. The Massachusetts Supreme Judicial Court is made up of a chief justice and six justices, appointed by the governor. They issue rulings regarding the appropriateness of the lower courts' decisions according to the principals of the state constitution.

Chapter 4

THE ECONOMY OF MASSACHUSETTS

The largest manufacturing industries in Massachusetts produce computers and electronic devices, scientific instruments, and other high-technology equipment. Massachusetts, especially in the greater Boston area, is a leader in the education and health care industries. The state is also a center for biotechnology and computer software development.

Education as an Industry

Higher education is a major industry in Massachusetts. Throughout Massachusetts there are more than seventy-five colleges and universities, with twenty-seven in the Boston area alone. Students come from all over the world to study in Massachusetts. Some of the best-known schools include Harvard University and the Massachusetts Institute of Technology (MIT) in Cambridge; Boston College, Boston University, Northeastern University, Suffolk University, the New England Conservatory of Music, and the University of Massachusetts in Boston; Clark University and the College of the Holy Cross in Worcester; Brandeis University in Waltham; and Tufts University in Medford.

These colleges and universities help make Massachusetts a leader in science and technology both through university-sponsored research and through the businesses started by many students who stay in Massachusetts after completing their education.

The Medical and Biotech Industries

The medical and health care industry plays a major role in the Massachusetts economy in two ways: through patient care facilities and the biotechnology industry. Massachusetts is home to more than 150 hospitals, many of them world famous. Among these are Massachusetts General Hospital, the Boston Children's Hospital, the Joslin Diabetes Center, the Dana Farber Cancer Institute in Boston,

The Baker Library, at the Harvard Business School, was founded in 1908 in Cambridge, Massachusetts.

and the Lahey Clinic in Burlington. People come from around the world to have their health problems treated in the Boston area. In addition, there are a number of universities in the state that have highly regarded medical schools, including Harvard University, Boston College, Tufts University, and the University of Massachusetts.

The combination of world-class hospitals and medical schools attracts a large amount of research money from private companies and government agencies like the National Institutes of Health (NIH).

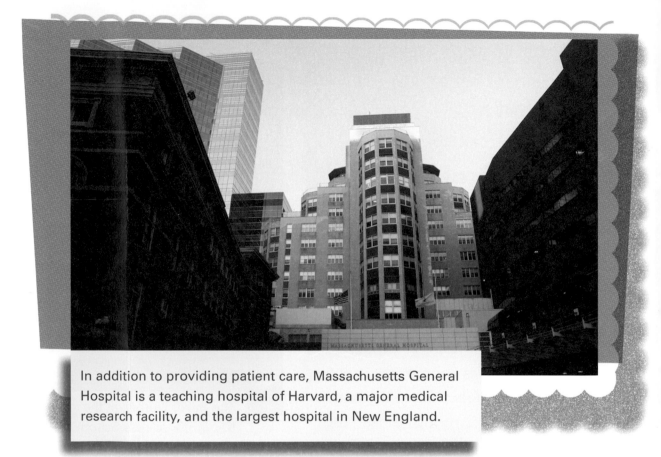

In addition to providing patient care, Massachusetts General Hospital is a teaching hospital of Harvard, a major medical research facility, and the largest hospital in New England.

As a result of this medical research, Massachusetts is a leader in biotechnology. Biotechnology uses techniques like genetic engineering (directly altering genes) to create new treatments for disease. Some of the most famous biotechnology companies in the country are located in Massachusetts, including Genzyme, Amgen, and Biogen.

High Technology

Biotechnology isn't the only scientific area in which Massachusetts excels. The Massachusetts Institute of Technology (MIT) has always

The Changing Economy

How people earned their living in Massachusetts has changed from century to century. When the first settlers arrived in Massachusetts, they made money not only by providing services to each other but also by trading with the home country, England. Settlers cut down trees and made masts, which were needed for the ships of the English navy. They also trapped animals and sent the furs back to England. The money they made from these exported goods was used to purchase manufactured goods like pottery and tea, which were shipped from England.

By the seventeenth century, Massachusetts had become a shipbuilding center. Its vessels sailed from the East Coast to all over the world, bringing back merchant goods. Massachusetts played a major role in the molasses-rum-slave trade. Merchants shipped in molasses from the West Indies. The molasses was used to make Boston baked beans—hence Boston's nickname, "Beantown." More important, molasses was distilled into rum, which was shipped to West Africa. The rum was traded for slaves, who were transported to the West Indies and sold to plantation owners. Plantation owners used the slaves to produce more molasses, which was shipped north to start the process all over again.

In the nineteenth century, the many rivers in Massachusetts provided power for factories that produced cloth and clothing, furniture, and shoes. In 1839, Charles Goodyear in Woburn developed the process of treating rubber with heat and sulfur to harden it, and started producing tires for bicycles and carriages.

Massachusetts played a leading role in providing services as well as goods. In 1782, the Harvard Medical School was formed. In 1811, Massachusetts General Hospital was created; it is the third-oldest hospital in the United States. In 1841, Boston-based department store chain Jordan Marsh was founded, and in 1862, the John Hancock Mutual Insurance Company was formed in Boston.

Today, relatively little manufacturing is done in Massachusetts. In general, the state has a service economy, with flourishing health care, education, engineering, and defense research and development industries.

Massachusetts's vast coastline is lined with beaches like this one. The state is home to a thriving resort industry around Cape Cod and the shore towns north of Boston.

turned out engineers and scientists who made major contributions to American technology. Massachusetts is home to thousands of companies engaged in developing computer software and hardware, scientific instruments, and advanced technologies for the aerospace and defense industries.

Tourism and Sports

Given the significant role that Massachusetts has played in American history, it's no surprise that tourism is a major industry. People from all over visit historic sites and museums located throughout the state. One of the most popular tourist attractions is the Freedom Trail in Boston, a 2.5-mile (4 km) walking tour that takes visitors past sixteen major historical sites. Two historical recreations are also popular. One of them, Plymouth Plantation, is a re-creation of the settlement of the Pilgrims in Plymouth. It includes period buildings and actors portraying people of the 1600s. A second attraction, Old Sturbridge Village in Sturbridge, re-creates a community as it would have been in the late 1700s to early 1800s.

History is not the only attraction that Massachusetts has to offer. Massachusetts is nicknamed "the Bay State" because it has a number of large bays along its coast. The Massachusetts coast is a popular resort area, especially the area around Cape Cod and the islands of Martha's Vineyard and Nantucket. For those interested in winter sports, the Berkshires, Wachusett Mountain, and the Nashoba Valley are popular skiing destinations.

Finally, Massachusetts is undeniably a sports center. The state hosts some of the country's most successful and popular professional sports teams. These include the New England Patriots football team, the Boston Celtics basketball team, the Boston Red Sox baseball team, and the Boston Bruins hockey team.

Perhaps the most famous sporting event in Boston is the Boston Marathon, the world's oldest annual marathon. It has been run since 1897. Organized by the Boston Athletic Association, it is run every April and attracts twenty thousand participants on average. Runners and spectators come from all over the world for the event.

Chapter 5

PEOPLE FROM MASSACHUSETTS:
PAST AND PRESENT

In its long history, Massachusetts has produced many people who have played a significant role in politics, social issues, science, and the arts. The following are some of the notable people from the state.

Politics

Samuel Adams (1722–1803) Samuel Adams was one of the leading patriots of the American Revolution. The son of a successful brewer in Quincy, Massachusetts, he devoted his life to American independence from Britain. Among his other activities, he masterminded the Boston Tea Party, in which patriots dumped a shipload of tea from England into Boston Harbor to protest the tax on it. After America declared independence, Adams, along with his cousin John Adams and James Bowdoin, wrote the Massachusetts Constitution.

John Adams (1735–1826) John Adams, born in Braintree, Massachusetts, was a patriot during the American Revolution. He played a major role in persuading the Continental Congress to adopt the Declaration of Independence and negotiating the peace treaty with Britain that ended the war. He was the United States' first vice president, under George Washington. In 1796, he became the second president of the United States.

John Quincy Adams (1767–1848) John Quincy Adams, also born in Braintree, was the son of John Adams. As secretary of state under President James Madison, he helped design the Monroe Doctrine. This policy forbade foreign powers from further colonizing the United States or interfering with U.S. affairs. In 1824, he was elected the sixth president of the United States.

Paul Revere (1735–1818)
Born in Boston, Paul Revere was a silversmith and maker of plates for printing. He risked arrest to warn leaders of the American Revolution about the invasion of the British army.

John F. Kennedy (1917–1963) Born in Brookline, Massachusetts, John F. Kennedy was elected the thirty-fifth U.S. president, in 1960. During his administration, the space program was begun and the civil rights movement became a major social force in

John F. Kennedy, born in Brookline, Massachusetts, was the thirty-fifth president of the United States.

African Americans in Massachusetts

African Americans have always played a vital role in Massachusetts. Crispus Attucks was the first black man to die in the American Revolution. In March 1770, a group of people had a confrontation with guards at the Boston customs house. Soldiers killed five colonists, among them Attucks. African American men participated in the Revolutionary War battles at Lexington and Concord, including Peter Salem, a freed slave, and Prince Estabrook, a slave who was wounded at Lexington and was later freed for his war service. At least twenty African Americans fought at the Battle of Bunker Hill.

In 1806, free blacks in Boston built the first African American church in America—the African Meeting House. In 1866, the first black legislators in America were elected to the Massachusetts legislature.

In 1900, Sergeant William H. Carney of the Massachusetts 54th Regiment received the Congressional Medal of Honor for rescuing the American flag and raising and keeping it aloft during the Battle of Fort Wagner in 1863. When he died in 1908, the state ordered all flags to be lowered to half-mast. That was the first time this had been done for an African American.

In 1967, Massachusetts became the first state to elect an African American to the U.S. Senate, Edward William Brooke III. In 2006, Deval Patrick became the first African American to be elected governor of Massachusetts.

This illustration shows the death of Crispus Attucks and four other men in 1770.

the United States. Kennedy was assassinated in Dallas, Texas, by Lee Harvey Oswald on November 22, 1963.

George H. W. Bush (1924–) George Bush Sr. was born in Milton, Massachusetts. He later moved to Texas and entered the oil business. From 1966 to 1980, he served as Texas congressman. In 1971, he became ambassador to the United Nations, and from 1980 to 1988, he was President Ronald Reagan's vice president. In 1988, he was elected the forty-first president of the United States.

Social Change

Susan B. Anthony (1820–1906) Susan Brownell Anthony was born near Adams, Massachusetts. She was a tireless campaigner for women's rights. As a suffragist, she played a key role in getting women the right to vote.

Clara Barton (1821–1912) Clara Barton was born in Oxford, Massachusetts. During the Civil War, she set up an organization to collect and distribute medical supplies for wounded soldiers. In 1881, she founded the American Red Cross. She based it on a similar organization she saw at work on battlefields in Europe in 1870, during the Franco-Prussian War.

Clara Barton modeled the American Red Cross on the International Committee of the Red Cross.

Science and Technology

Charles Bullfinch (1763–1841) Born in Boston, Charles Bullfinch was an architect who created the Federal style, in which domes and columns are used to create formal, elegant buildings. Among his works are the U.S. Capitol in Washington, D.C., and Faneuil Hall and the statehouse in Boston.

Luther Burbank (1849–1926) Born in Lancaster, Massachusetts, Luther Burbank was a botanist (a scientist who studies plants). In the course of his career, he developed eight hundred different species of plants.

Samuel F. B. Morse (1791–1872) Born in Charlestown, Massachusetts, Samuel Morse was an inventor. He is best known for inventing the telegraph and Morse code. In the days before telephones, the telegraph revolutionized communication by allowing messages to be sent instantly over electric wires across long distances.

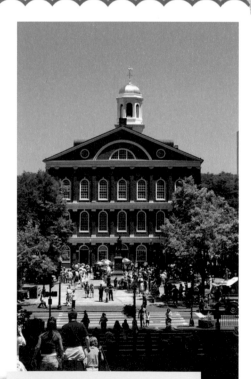

Boston's Faneuil Hall was the meeting place of colonial patriots. Today, it is a popular tourist attraction.

The Arts

Emily Dickinson (1830–1886) Famous poet Emily Dickinson

was born in Amherst, Massachusetts. Her poetry is unique and often inspired by nature and personal experience, rather than great events.

Ralph Waldo Emerson (1802–1883) Born in Boston, Ralph Waldo Emerson was a philosopher and author who wrote essays and poetry. He is known for promoting the philosophy of transcendentalism. Transcendentalism is the idea that people should do what is natural and seek enlightenment through their own inner senses, rather than from religious authorities.

Nathaniel Hawthorne (1804–1864) Born in Salem, Massachusetts, Nathaniel Hawthorne was a novelist. His most widely read works are *The Scarlet Letter* and *The House of the Seven Gables*.

Dr. Seuss (Theodore Geisel) (1904–1991) Born in Springfield, Massachusetts, Theodore Geisel wrote more than sixty children's books. His books feature quirky illustrations and rhyming text. Among them are *The Cat in the Hat*, *Green Eggs and Ham*, and *How the Grinch Stole Christmas*.

Dr. Seuss wrote *The Cat in the Hat* in response to a *Life* magazine article on the lack of interesting books for schoolchildren.

Henry David Thoreau (1817–1862) Born in Concord, Massachusetts, Henry David Thoreau was a philosopher and author. He believed that individuals should resist a government that they felt was unjust. He is best known for writing *Walden; or, Life in the Woods*. This book recounts his experience of spending two years living a simple life in a small house in the forest near Walden Pond in Concord, Massachusetts.

James Abbott McNeill Whistler (1834–1903) Born in Lowell, Massachusetts, Whistler was a painter who promoted the idea of "art for art's sake." His most famous work is the portrait of his mother, titled *Arrangement in Gray and Black*. It is more commonly known as *Whistler's Mother*.

Timeline

1620	The Pilgrims arrive at Plymouth.
1629	The Puritans establish the Massachusetts Bay Company and settle Boston.
1636	Harvard College is established.
1775	The first battle of the Revolutionary War takes place at Lexington.
1788	Massachusetts becomes the sixth state to ratify the U.S. Constitution.
1824	John Quincy Adams is elected sixth president of the United States.
1832	William Lloyd Garrison starts the New England Anti-Slavery Society.
1891	The first basketball game takes place in Springfield.
1892–1893	J. Frank Duryea creates the first fully functioning gas-powered automobile in Springfield.
1898	The first subway system in the United States starts operating in Boston.
1925	Edith Nourse Rogers becomes the first woman to serve in the U.S. House of Representatives.
1944	Howard Allan of Harvard University develops the first digital computer.
1947	Raytheon Corporation invents the first microwave oven; Edwin Land invents the Polaroid camera; Sydney Farber develops the first chemo-therapy treatment for cancer.
1960	John F. Kennedy is elected thirty-fifth president of the United States.
1974	Desegregation of the Boston school system is carried out at the order of the federal government.
1991–2007	Construction takes place on "the Big Dig," a massive highway development in Boston.

State motto	*Ense petit placidam sub libertate quietem* ("By the sword we seek peace, but peace only under liberty.")
State capital	Boston
State flower	Mayflower (*trailing arbutus*) (*Epigaea repens*)
State bird	Black-capped chickadee (*Parus atricapillus*)
State game bird	Wild turkey (*Meleagris gallopavo*)
State dog	Boston terrier (*Canis familiaris bostenensis*)
State song	"All Hail to Massachusetts"
State tree	American elm (*Ulmus americana*)
State book	*Make Way for Ducklings*, by Robert McCloskey
Statehood date and number	1788, sixth state
State nickname	"The Bay State"
Total area and U.S. rank	10,555 square miles (27,337 square km), forty-fourth largest state

State Flag

State Seal

Approximate population at most recent census	6,450,000
Length of coastline	1,500 miles (2,400 kilometers)
Highest elevation	Mt. Greylock, 3,491 feet (1,064 meters)
Lowest elevation	Sea level, at the Atlantic Ocean
Major rivers	Charles River, Merrimack River, Connecticut River
Highest temperature recorded	107°F (41.7°C), August 2, 1975, at Chester and New Bedford
Lowest temperature recorded	−35°F (−37°C), January 12, 1981, at Chester.
Origin of state name	Native American word for "place of great hills"
Chief agricultural products	Cranberries, corn, apples
Major industries	Electronics, biotechnology, health care, fishing, tourism, education

State Bird

State Flower

GLOSSARY

abolitionist Person who wanted to abolish slavery, especially in the United States.

biotechnology The field in which advanced technology is used to create medical treatments.

conservation Maintenance and protection of the environment and the species in it.

Continental navy The official navy of the thirteen colonies during the Revolutionary War.

delegate A person chosen to represent a group at a convention.

genetic engineering The field that focuses on directly changing the genes in an organism.

Great Depression The period from 1929 to the late 1930s during which the United States experienced a terrible economic downturn.

immigrate To enter one country after leaving another.

Industrial Revolution Period from the end of the eighteenth century through the nineteenth century when machines replaced hand tools as the means of making goods.

persecution The act of picking on or punishing people because of their beliefs or other characteristics.

precipitation Rain and snow.

privateer Ship given permission by a government to engage in piracy against enemy ships.

ratify To formally agree to.

suffragist A person, often a woman, who tries to obtain the right to vote for those who don't have it, usually other women.

temperate climate A climate with four distinct seasons.

textile Cloth.

Boston Historical Society

206 Washington Street

Boston, MA 02109

(617) 720-1713

Web site: http://www.bostonhistory.org

This organization maintains a history museum and the Old Statehouse Museum, and provides a variety of written resources.

Freedom Trail Foundation

99 Chauncy Street, Suite 401

Boston, MA 02111

(617) 357-8300

Web site: http://www.thefreedomtrail.org

This organization provides information for self-guided and escorted tours of the Freedom Trail. Its Web site contains resources for students and teachers.

Lowell National Historic Park

246 Market Street

Lowell, MA 01862

(987) 970-5000

Web site: http://www.nps.gov/lowe

This park contains buildings and exhibits relating to the textile trade and Massachusetts during the Industrial Revolution.

Massachusetts Archives

220 William T. Morrissey Boulevard

Boston, MA 02125

(617) 727-2816

Web site: http://www.sec.state.ma.us/arc

This organization maintains historic documents that can be used for research. It also maintains the Commonwealth Museum, which contains historical exhibits.

Massachusetts Historical Society

1154 Boylston Street

Boston, MA 02215

(617) 536-1608

Web site: http://www.masshist.org/welcome

This organization, founded in 1791, provides a variety of online resources and publications on Massachusetts history, as well as a library.

New Bedford Whaling Museum

18 Johnny Cake Hill

New Bedford, MA

(508) 997-0046

Web site: http://www.museumsofboston.org/museums/newbedfordwhaling.html

Located in New Bedford Whaling National Park, this museum houses the world's most comprehensive collection of whaling artifacts.

Old Sturbridge Village

1 Sturbridge Village Road

Sturbridge, MA 01566

(800) 733-1830

Web site: http://www.osv.org

This organization maintains a full-scale reproduction of a late-eighteenth/early-nineteenth–century community.

Plimouth Plantation

137 Warren Avenue

Plymouth, MA 02360

(508) 763-1622

Web site: http://www.plimoth.org

This organization maintains a full-scale reproduction of a seventeenth-century community.

Salem Witch Museum

Washington Square North

Salem, MA 01970

(978) 744-1692

Web site: http://www.salemwitchmuseum.com

This museum chronicles the Salem witch trials.

USS *Constitution*

24 5th Street

Charlestown, MA 02129

(617) 242-5670

Web site: http://www.ussconstitution.navy.mil

The USS *Constitution* is the famous "Old Ironsides" ship from the American Revolution. It can be toured by visitors and also includes an adjacent museum.

Web Sites

Due to the changing nature of Internet links, Rosen Publishing has developed an online list of Web sites related to the subject of this book. This site is updated regularly. Please use this link to access the list:

http://www.rosenlinks.com/uspp/mapp

For Further Reading

Burgan, Michael. *Voices from Colonial America: Massachusetts 1620–1776*. Des Moines, IA: National Geographic Children's Books, 2005.

Cox, Clinton. *Undying Glory: The Story of the Massachusetts 54th Regiment*. Bloomington, IN: BackinPrint.com/iUniverse, 2007.

Freedman, Jeri. *A Primary Source History of the Colony of Massachusetts*. New York, NY: Rosen Publishing Group, 2005.

Grace, Catherine O'Neill, Peter Aernstam, and John Kemp. *Mayflower 1620: A New Look at a Pilgrim Voyage*. Los Angeles, CA: National Geographic, 2003.

Hinman, Bonnie. *The Massachusetts Bay Colony: The Puritans Arrive in New England*. Hockessin, DE: Mitchell Lane, 2008.

McNulty, Elizabeth. *Boston Then and Now*. San Diego, CA: Thunder Bay Press, 2002.

Rappaport, Doreen, Greg Call, and Joan Verniero. *Victory or Death!: Stories of the American Revolution*. New York, NY: HarperCollins, 2003.

Sanmarco, Anthony Mitchell. *Boston's Back Bay in the Victorian Era*. Mt. Pleasant, SC: Arcadia Publishing, 2003.

BIBLIOGRAPHY

Allison, Robert J. *A Short History of Boston*. Beverly, MA: Commonwealth Editions, 2004.

AmericanRevolution.com. "African Americans in the Revolutionary Period." 1996–2005. Retrieved October 30, 2008 (http://www.americanrevolution.com/ AfricanAmericansInTheRevolution.htm).

Brown, Richard, and Jack Tager. *A Concise History of Massachusetts*. Boston, MA: University of Massachusetts, 2000.

Commonwealth of Massachusetts. "Understanding the Structure of State Government." Retrieved October 15, 2008 (http://www.mass.gov/?pageID = mg2terminal&L = 3&L0 = Home&L1 = State + Government&L2 = About + State + Government&sid = massgov2&b = terminalcontent&f = understand_structure_of_stategov&csid = massgov2).

Commonwealth of Massachusetts Citizen Information Services. "Miscellaneous Massachusetts Facts: Massachusetts Firsts." Retrieved October 12, 2008 (http:// www.sec.state.ma.us/cis/cismaf/mf4.htm).

Gross, Robert A. *The Minutemen and Their World*. New York, NY: Hill & Wang, 2001.

Logan, Samuel T., Jr. "The Pilgrims and Puritans: Total Reformation for the Glory of God." Retrieved October 13, 2008 (http://www.puritansermons.com/banner/logan1.htm).

Massachusetts Department of Fish and Game. "Massachusetts Wildlife." Retrieved October 14, 2008 (http://www.mass.gov/dfwele/dfw/wildlife/wildlife_home.htm).

NativeAmericans.com. "Wampanoag." 2007. Retrieved December 5, 2008 (http://www. nativeamericans.com/Wampanoag.htm).

NYTimes.com. "First Trolley Car from Boston Here; Street Railway Men on a Junket Have Rails Laid to Bridge a Gap." *New York Times*, March 22, 1912. Retrieved October 30, 2008 (http://query.nytimes.com/gst/abstract.html?res = 9D0DEFDC1F31E233A25751C2A9659C946396D6CF).

O'Connor, Thomas H. *Bibles, Brahmins, and Bosses*. Boston, NY: Boston Public Library, 1991.

Ross, Marjorie Drake. *The Book of Boston: The Victorian Period 1837–1901*. New York, NY: Hasting House Publishers, 1964.

U.S. Army. "A Chronology of African American Military Service from the Civil War to World War I." Retrieved October 14, 2008 (http://www.redstone.army.mil/history/ integrate/chron2.htm).

U.S. Census Bureau. "State and County Quick Facts: Massachusetts." Retrieved October 12, 2008 (http://quickfacts.census.gov/qfd/states/25000.html).

Weather.com. "Climate for Massachusetts." 2003–2007. Retrieved October 13, 2008 (http://www.rssweather.com/climate/Massachusetts/Boston/#temp).

INDEX

47

About the Author

Jeri Freedman has a B.A. from Harvard University. She is the author of more than twenty-five young adult nonfiction books, many of them published by Rosen Publishing. Freedman's previous titles include *A Primary Source History of the Colony of Massachusetts*; *Hillary Rodham Clinton: Portrait of a Leading Democrat*; *Armenian Genocide*; and *American Debates: Privacy vs. Security*. She lives in Boston, Massachusetts.

Photo Credits

Cover (top, left) © www.istockphoto.com/Steven Wynn; cover (top, right) © www.istockphoto.com/photo168; cover (bottom), pp. 22 (right), 28, 40 (right), 41 Wikimedia Commons; pp. 1, 3, 6, 12, 21, 26, 32, 39 © www.istockphoto.com/Karen Brockney; p. 4 (top) © GeoAtlas; p. 7 © www.istockphoto.com/Denis Jr. Tangney; pp. 8, 36 © www.istockphoto.com/Jorge Salcedo; p. 11 Courtesy of Basketball Hall of Fame; pp. 13, 35 Library of Congress Prints and Photographs Division; pp. 15, 30 © Rick Friedman/Corbis; p. 16 Réunion des Musées Nationaux/Art Resource, NY; p. 19 krtphotos/Newscom.com; p. 20 John Coletti/The Image Bank/Getty Images; p. 22 (left) © www.istockphoto.com/Stephen Orsillo; p. 24 Wikipedia; p. 27 Shutterstock.com; pp. 33, 34 © Bettmann/Corbis; p. 37 Gene Lester/Hulton Archive/Getty Images; p. 40 (left) Courtesy of Robesus, Inc.

Designer: Les Kanturek; Photo Researcher: Amy Feinberg